BETWEEN
WARM-UP&WORSHIP
Prayers for Choirs on the Run

James H. Smylie
Edited by Mary Nelson Keithahn

Abingdon Press
Nashville

BETWEEN WARM-UP AND WORSHIP: PRAYERS FOR CHOIRS ON THE RUN

Copyright © 1998 by Abingdon Press

This book is printed on acid-free, recycled paper.

ISBN 0-687-08830-5

Scripture quotations are from the New Revised Standard Version Bible, copyright © 1989 by the Division of Christian Education of the National Council of the Churches of Christ in the USA.

98 99 00 01 02 03 04 05 06 07—10 9 8 7 6 5 4 3 2 1

Manufactured in the United States of America

Preface

For many years, I have been singing with my wife, Elizabeth R. Smylie, in the choir at Ginter Park Presbyterian Church in Richmond, Virginia, under the direction of organist/director David McCormick, Professor of Sacred Music at the Presbyterian School of Christian Education (retired). During that time, I have frequently been asked to pray with the choir before we enter the sanctuary for worship. The choir's positive response has encouraged me to revise and refine my prayers for this collection, which is designed for use by pastors, choir directors, organists, and others who are also called to pray with the choir "between warm-up and worship."

The subtitle for this collection, "Prayers for Choirs on the Run," may be subject to some misinterpretation. Some may think it refers to choirs who may, at times, seek divine protection from a congregation disgruntled over anthems not prepared well enough, singing too sharp or flat for their ears, a new hymn that has not been properly introduced, or an anthem in an unfamiliar musical style. The Ginter Park choir has had to seek such protection from time to time! Instead, the subtitle refers to situations in which most choirs find themselves before a service: practicing until the last minute, rushing to robe, and hurrying to the choir loft, with little time to pray. Pastors also find themselves "on the run," dealing with last-minute preparations or interruptions, and trying to compose themselves as well as an appropriate prayer for the choir. I know because I have had to face these hectic moments in the life of a choir.

It is my hope that this collection of prayers will give persons who pray with choirs a new sensitivity and awareness of the importance of music for praising God in the Christian community, and serve as a model for them to use in composing their own prayers. Keep in mind that these prayers are prayers for the choir, not all-purpose prayers. I have written them to help choirs focus on their main purpose, which is to assist pastors and the congregation in the divine worship of God. I have also taken into consideration the liturgical and calendar years, and the special situations and occasions in the life of a congregation, as well as the need for God's people to give thanks, lament, cry for help, and seek guidance and inspiration. In writing the prayers, I have drawn on life, scripture, hymns and anthems, larger choral works, poetry, literature, theological writings, and other worship resources. I have tried to keep most of the prayers focused on a single theme appropriate for the day, and short and simple enough for easy adaptation to other settings. The indexes of scripture, psalm, and hymn references will be useful in congregations that use the lectionary.

I wish to express thanks to Sally Hicks, Norma T. Kuhn, Katherine R. Davis, and Jill F. Torbett who patiently transcribed these prayers over the years. I would also like to express gratitude to Mary Nelson Keithahn whose editorial skills, insights, and enthusiasm made this volume a reality.

This volume is dedicated to my spouse, Elizabeth, whose own love of music has enriched our life together for over forty-five years. It is also dedicated to the choirs of the Ginter Park Presbyterian Church, who have meant so much to us and our family, and to the congregation with whom we have worshiped God for so many years.

James H. Smylie
Professor of Church History, Emeritus
Union Theological Seminary
Richmond, Virginia

Contents

Fall

Winter

Spring

Summer

Indexes

Fall
Prayers of Praise and Thanksgiving

1 A Responsive Prayer

Leader: Make a joyful noise to God, all the earth!
Choir: Worship God with gladness!
Leader: Come into God's presence with singing!
Choir: Enter into God's house with praise!
Leader: Bless God! God's name be praised!
Choir: Bless God! God's name be praised!

(Adapted from Psalm 100)

2

Let the heights of heaven adore you,
angel hosts, your praises sing.
Let powers, dominions bow before you,
and every voice in concert ring.
Let no tongue on earth be silent,
as we praise you, God and King.
Amen.

(Adapted from "Of the Father's Love Begotten," by Aurelius Clemens Prudentius,
A.D. 348–413; trans. John Mason Neale, 1854, and Henry Williams Baker, 1859)

3 Litany

God, we belong to you.
Let your Word inform our singing.
God, we belong to you.
Let your Spirit inspire our singing.
God, we belong to you.
Let our lips sing your praises.
God, we belong to you.
Let us live and die to you.
Let the choir sing:
Amen.

(Inspired by John Calvin, 1509–1564)

4

Creator God, the heavens sing of your glory,
and the whole earth sings of the work of your hands!
Who are we, and what is our music
that you should pay attention to us!
We are your people, God,
made after your image—
sopranos, tenors, altos, basses—
with the words and notes
you have put into our hearts and mouths.
So hear us as we give praise for our redemption,
and unite our voices with the songs
of your whole creation.
In the name of Christ, your New Creation,
we sing and pray.
Amen.

(Inspired by Psalms 8 and 19)

5

Lord Jesus,
It is you who called us here.
It is as your choir we sing.
It is to your people we minister.
It is your inspiration we need.
It is your service we seek.
So satisfy us, Lord Jesus.
Amen.

6

Great Director,
we are through rehearsing now.
Help us to be still
and remember that you are God.
Out of that stillness
bring forth music
inspired by your Word and Holy Spirit,
that will stir our congregation
to join us in praising you
and rejoicing in your power and presence.
In Christ's name, we sing.
Amen.

(Inspired by Psalm 46:10)

7

God of all times and places,
this morning we sing
the words of the psalmist
and the music of Felix Mendelssohn.
We give thanks
that you do not
slumber or sleep
but still watch over us,
as you did over Israel.
Awaken us from our slumbers
by your Word and Spirit
that we may be ever watch-full
and care-full of one another
and your creation.
In Christ's name, we sing.
Amen.

(Inspired by Psalm 121:4;
and "He, Watching Over Israel" from *Elijah* by Felix Mendelssohn, 1809–1847)

8

Oh, for a thousand tongues to sing your praise,
Great Redeemer—
tongues of fruitfulness, love and joy,
tongues of gentleness and self-control,
tongues of patience and peace—
all the triumphs of your grace,
the music of our grateful lives.
Let the choir sing:
Amen and Amen.

(Adapted from "O For a Thousand Tongues to Sing," by Charles Wesley, 1738)

9

Creator, Redeemer, Provider God,
who is like unto you
who delivers us from the idols of this world?
With the House of Moses and Miriam,
With the House of Mary and Joseph,
let the House of McCormick* praise your name,
let the House of Frank praise your name,
let the House of Bedsole praise your name,
let the House of Benson praise your name,
let the House of Jung praise your name,
let the House of Lumpkin praise your name,
let the House of Mottley praise your name,
let the House of Dale praise your name,
Let all our Houses praise you this day.
Let the choir say:
Amen and Amen.

(*Insert the last names of your choir families in each acclamation.)

(Inspired by Psalm 135:19-21)

10

How good it is to sing your praises,
Most High God,
and to thank you for your gracious gifts.
Continue to show your faithfulness
and loving-kindness
to us and our congregation today.
In Christ's name, Amen.

(Adapted from Psalm 147:1)

11

Let us praise God:
Praise God in this sanctuary!
Praise God for great and mighty deeds!
Praise God with our voices—
soprano, tenor, alto, bass!
Praise God with every breath of life!
Praise God for Jesus Christ our Lord,
in whose name we pray.
Amen.

(Adapted from Psalm 150)

12

God, Source of all that we have and are,
you have made us for yourself,
and we are restless
until we find our rest in you.
We praise you for the music
that consoles us,
comforts us,
challenges us in our restlessness,
as we journey through life
with Christ, our companion,
in whose name we sing and pray.
Amen.

(Adapted from *Confessions* by Augustine of Hippo, A.D. 354–430)

13

Creator God,
keep us from vain show
as we sing this Vaughan Williams* anthem.
Rather, by the power of your Word and Spirit,
use our music to help your congregation
in this corner of the world
shout of your glory
and express our gratitude for your awesome universe.
So let our praises grow.
Alleluia!
Amen.

(* Substitute the name of the composer/arranger of the day's anthem.)

14

Almighty God,
your thoughts are high above our thoughts,
your ways above our ways,
your music above our poor efforts to sing.
Yet you have called us into your presence
to sing your praise.
Inspire our singing by your Word and Spirit;
be as near to us as the air we breathe,
that all the world
may discern your will,
walk in your way,
and join in our songs of praise.
In Christ's name, we pray.
Amen.

15

O Son of God, the source of life,
Praise is your due by night and day.
Our happy lips must raise the strain
of your esteemed and splendid name.
Amen.

(From "O Radiant Light, O Sun Divine" [Phos Hilaron],
third-century song translated by William G. Storey, ca. 1970)

16

God, Source of all our melodies and harmonies,
accept our praise offering this day.
Let the horizontal notes we sing
convey the simple message
of your love for the world and each of us;
the vertical notes,
the richness of your love
that meets our every need.
So may our music
carry your Word and Spirit
into the hearts and lives
of all who worship here.
We sing in Christ's name.
Amen.

17

Gifted by you, God, we turn to you,
offering up ourselves in praise;
thankful songs shall rise forever,
Gracious Giver of our days.
Amen.

(Adapted from "God, Whose Giving Knows No Ending,"
by Robert L. Edwards, 1961)

18

God of all notes from A to G:
We can sing in F sharp.
We can sing in C.
Does it mean a thing to you,
or should we change the key?
Would you listen to our song
if we sang A flat?
We would change it all for you
if that is where it's at.
We believe in praising.
We believe it, true.
We believe each note we raise.
We trust we're getting through!
Amen.

(Adapted from *Mass*, by Leonard Bernstein)

19

What do you require of us, God?
With what shall we come before you?
Today we come with praise,
not just with notes and words,
rhythm and dynamics alone,
but with humble and contrite hearts,
dedicating ourselves
to more compassionate and just lives.
Give to us, God, what it is that you require,
in Christ's name.
Amen.

(Inspired by Micah 6:6)

Prayers Asking God's Presence and Guidance

20

Divine Musician,
on this first day of the week,
give us faith, hope and love
that we may move
to the rhythm
of your will and ways
following in the steps of Jesus,
in whose name we sing.
Amen.

21

Mighty and magnanimous God,
you are not confined
to buildings of wood and brick and stone,
filled with priests and preachers and choirs.
Your dwelling place is the whole earth
and in our hearts.
We gather as your people
in this particular place,
at your bidding,
to pray for your presence,
listen to your word,
praise you for your goodness,
and rededicate ourselves
to your service in the world.
So visit us, God,
we pray,
in Christ's name.
Amen.

(Inspired by Psalm 90:1)

22

Loving God,
inspire our music by your Word and Holy Spirit,
that we may sing our part
as though we may never sing again,
as needy women and men
to needy women and men,
to satisfy every longing heart.
In Christ's name, we sing.
Amen.

(Adapted from *The Reformed Pastor*, by Richard Baxter)

23

Before we raise our voices in praise, God,
we bow our heads and hearts in prayer.
Lift our eyes that we may see you.
Lift our heads that we may know you.
Lift our hearts that we may sing your love
not only with our voices,
but with our lives, in Christ's name.
Amen.

24

Inspire us today, God,
in our ministry of music.
We have practiced
breathing in, breathing out,
breathing in, breathing out,
breathing in, breathing out.
Now let your Word and Spirit
refresh and renew us,
making every breath we breathe
an ode of joy to you.
Let the choir sing,
Amen.

25

As we begin a new week, God,
we return to you,
our Center.
Use our gathering,
preaching,
listening,
praying, singing
to refocus our life on you,
and because of you,
on one another
and the world you love.
In Christ's name, we sing.
Amen.

26

Faithful God,
today we sing our anthems *a cappella*,
but that does not mean
we sing without your accompaniment.
Accompany us in our ministry of music,
and accompany this congregation
in our worship and service in the world.
So sing with us,
Faithful God,
sing with us.
Amen.

27

God of all words and melodies,
may the songs we sing today in worship
go with us on our journey of faith
in the week ahead.
Give us upright songs,
that no unworthy affection may drag us down;
steadfast songs,
that no unworthy purpose may lead us astray;
triumphant songs,
that no trial or tribulation
may dampen or destroy our spirits.
With such songs,
help us to worship you with our lives,
as well as our lips.
Let all the people say, Amen.

28

What does it profit us
or this congregation, Lord,
if we sing like
Metropolitan Opera stars,
and have not love?
Let your Word and Holy Spirit
fill our singing with love,
the greatest of your gifts
and the source of our praise.
In the name of Love, we pray.
Amen.

(Inspired by Matthew 16:26 and 1 Corinthians 13)

29

God, our God,
lift our hearts and tune our ears and voices
to your servants Elijah and Mendelssohn.
Speak to us through earthquake, wind, and fire
as we sing *fortissimo*, even double *fortissimo*.
Speak to us through the still small voice
as we sing *pianissimo*, even double *pianissimo*.
Speak to us through the sound of silence.
Help us—director, singers, and instrumentalists all—
to seek to know you with all our hearts,
and walk together in your way. Amen.

(Inspired by *Elijah*, by Felix Mendelssohn, 1809–1847)

30

God, Ruler of all being,
in the middle of our
hum-drum, ho-hum lives,
we pause to sing with the angels,
"Holy, holy, holy God,
the whole earth is full of your glory."
May this music
deliver us from our doldrums
and open our eyes to your glory,
to the wonders of your creation,
to the troubles of the world.
Give us, as you gave Isaiah,
the vision,
the will,
the voice to make a difference.
So inspire us this day. Amen.

(Inspired by Isaiah 6)

31

God,
today we approach you once more
filled with awe by the mystic chords of music.
Give us the grace to understand the meaning of this
big, booming, buzzing, mysterious life
that stirs us to sing,
"Holy, holy, holy God"
in the name of Jesus the Christ.
Amen.

(Inspired by "Holy, Holy, Holy! Lord God Almighty,"
by Reginald Heber, 1783–1826)

32

God,
you have taught us
to sing justice,
to sing compassion,
to sing humbly
before you.
Help us so
to sing and live
in Christ's name.
Amen.

(Inspired by Micah 6:8)

33

All-knowing, compassionate God,
you know our heart of hearts
and our mood today:
Some of us sing from conviction,
some from convention;
some of us are certain,
some uncertain.
Some of us come with
good conscience and bad;
with belief,
half-belief,
and disbelief.
Embrace us all by your love song
in whatever condition you find us.
Draw us to firmer faith,
and fuller service
in your kingdom.
In Christ's name, we offer praise to you.
Amen.

(Adapted from Karl Barth, 1886–1968)

34

Almighty God,
as you kindled the burning bush
and spoke to your servant, Moses,
so kindle your fire
in our hearts and in our music,
that this congregation
may hear your word
and know your love,
made known in Christ Jesus.
Amen.

(Inspired by Exodus 3:1-6)

Prayers for Others

35

God, Fountain of life,
today we seek refreshment
from your Word and Spirit.
Satisfy our thirst,
especially those whose spirits are dry and dusty,
who need a taste of that living water, Jesus Christ,
in whose name we drink and sing.
Amen.

(Inspired by John 4:7-26)

36

We think we are "with it" today, God,
singing this ancient psalm of praise
in this modern musical idiom.
We want the congregation to "get with it" too,
so let your Spirit be in our singing
that they may hear your Word
and be able to worship you in spirit and in truth.
Come, Holy Spirit, come.
Amen.

37

God of every troubled heart,
on this Lord's day
use our singing
to meet the needs
of your sorrowing, sighing, crying people
and help us see
that every day is your day.
Let the choir sing:
Amen.

38

Righteous God,
still every song within us
that is not your own,
so that what
and how
we sing today
may be for the health and welfare
of this congregation and the whole world,
all of which belongs to you.
In Christ's name, we sing.
Amen.

39

God of healing,
blend our voices
that the hymns and anthems we sing
may be balm from Gilead
for each person gathered here
who faces sadness, sickness, even death.
Especially be a balm to Russell,*
and restore him to his family,
and to this choir,
that he may blend his voice again with ours.
In Christ's name we pray.
Amen.

(* Substitute the name of a choir member who is ill.)

(Inspired by Jeremiah 8:22 and "There Is a Balm in Gilead, "
African American spiritual)

40

God of Everywoman and Everyman,
let our music this day
minister to everyone who needs you.
Help us sing:
  dolcissimo for those whose lives have gone sour;
  allegro for those who have had to slow down;
  andante for those whose lives are going too fast;
  pianissimo for those who find the noise of the world
    too loud;
  largamento for those who need a larger vision of life;
  forte for those who have lost their courage.
Embrace us, everyone, with that love
which the world cannot give or take away,
even Jesus Christ, our Lord.
Amen.

Prayers of Commitment and Dedication

41

God of all being,
Take our voices, let them sing
always, only, for you, King.
Take our lips and make them true,
filled with messages from you.
Amen.

(Adapted from "Take My Life and Let It Be Consecrated,"
by Frances R. Havergal, 1874)

42

Holy God,
whose service is our life,
let our songs
come into your presence as incense;
the lifting up of our voices
as a morning sacrifice.
In the name of Jesus,
our great high priest, we pray.
Amen.

(Inspired by Psalm 141:2)

43

Let all the songs of our hearts,
our words and notes,
the rhythms of our mouths and bodies,
be acceptable to you, God,
our Strength and Redeemer.
Amen.

(Inspired by Psalm 19:14)

44

To know you, God, is life.
To serve you, is perfect freedom.
To praise you with a life of service and song,
is our soul's joy.
As we pray, so let us sing and live, in Christ's name.
Amen.

45

Creator God,
we thank you for music.
Just as you divided
light from darkness,
water from dry land,
male from female,
so you divided
voice from voice,
note from note.
Take our different
voices and notes—
soprano and tenor,
alto and bass—
and, by the power
of your Word and Spirit,
make music to satisfy
the yearnings and strivings
of this congregation
after your benediction.
In Christ's name, we pray and sing.
Amen.

(Inspired by Genesis 1:1—2:4)

Special Days and Seasons

46 Labor Day

Ever-present God,
let songs from your great heart
sing in the hearts of every Christian,
that in our sitting down and rising up,
our solitude and society,
our labor and leisure
our getting and giving,
in every condition,
we may all know your presence
and serve you and one another
with our whole hearts.
In the name of Christ, our fellow worker, we sing.
Amen.

47 Singing from a New Hymnal

Today, God, we sing music from our new hymnal,
music from the four corners of the earth,
from many different experiences and tongues,
but with one purpose, to praise you.
So unite our voices
with Christian sisters and brothers the world over,
that the whole earth may rejoice in your
creative, redemptive, providential purposes.
Come, Holy Spirit, come.
Amen.

48 A Hymn Festival

God, we thank you for the great choir of witnesses
from every tradition and regions of the earth
that we meet in our hymnal.
We praise you for Hebrew psalms.
We praise you for Orthodox psalms.
We praise you for Roman Catholic psalms.
We praise you for Protestant psalms.
We praise you for African psalms.
We praise you for Latin American psalms.
We praise you for Native American psalms.
We praise you for Asian psalms.
Unite our hearts and voices,
enrich our worship, and
strengthen our witness
to the peoples of your one world.
We pray in Christ's name.
Amen.

(Inspired by Hebrews 12:1)

49 Hymn Festival or Hymnal Dedication

God of many songs,
we celebrate our hymnbook today,
borrowing Christian songs of praise
from every continent and nation of the earth.
We rejoice that you have called us to be part of
the one, holy, catholic, apostolic family
that is the church.
Lead us in our celebration,
as we sing and pray in the name of Jesus Christ,
the great head of that church.
Amen.

50 Choir Festival or Ecumenical Service

God in Christ,
bless us as we join our voices
with choirs in this community
and throughout the world
to praise your holy name.
Make us faithful troubadours,
and speak your Word through us,
that others may hear us as one great chorus
witnessing to Jesus Christ,
in whose name we sing.
Amen.

51 World Communion Sunday

God of all peoples,
on this World Communion Sunday,
the sun never sets on your
choirs and congregations
as we gather at the Lord's Table
to share bread and the fruit of the vine.
Unite our voices with theirs, we pray,
that we might witness to your love
in Jesus Christ
for the whole world.
Amen.

52 World Communion Sunday

God of the one and the many,
as we gather around the Lord's Table today,
we pray that your Word and Spirit
will unite us with Christ,
and with one another
so that when we join our voices in praise,
we will be as one people with a single voice,
witnessing to the world of your grace
and our common hope in Christ.
Amen.

53 Communion

Generous God,
you provided manna and water in the wilderness
for Moses and your wandering, complaining people.
Provide for us, we pray,
by your Word and Spirit
and through this bread and wine,
refreshment and strength for our pilgrimage
through these bewildering times.
Give us songs of gratitude in our hearts
and new directions for our journey,
that we may continue in your way without complaint,
guided by Christ, our constant companion,
in whose name we pray and sing.
Amen.

(Inspired by Exodus 16)

54 Reformation Sunday or All Saints' Day

God, you are our God!
With the whole company of angels,
the cherubim and seraphim,
we praise you.
With the glorious company of apostles,
we praise you.
With the goodly fellowship of prophets,
we praise you.
With the noble army of martyrs,
we praise you.
With the communion of the saints,
we praise you.
With our congregation and choir,
we praise you.
God, accept our praise this day.
Amen.

(Adapted from the "Te Deum Laudamus," fourth century)

55 Thanksgiving Day

Bounteous God,
our song today is one of thanksgiving
for full harvests, full tables,
and full stomachs.
We know that we do not live
by turkey and dressing alone,
but by your Word.
So fill us with your Spirit
that we may use our fullness and bounty
to help those who are hungry

and have little cause to feel grateful at all.
We pray and sing in the name
of Jesus Christ, the Bread of Life.
Amen.

(Inspired by Matthew 4:1-4 and John 6:35)

56 Thanksgiving Day

God, Giver of all that we enjoy,
on this Thanksgiving Day
we offer our hymns and anthems
in gratitude for your goodness to us.
We are a people of plenty and pleasure, God.
Keep us from being so stuffed with turkey, dressing,
and football
that we forget those who are
hungry, homeless, jobless,
and anxious about their prospects.
Inspire us through our music
to responsible living
that all your people may enjoy
the bounty of this season.
Let the choir sing:
Amen.

57 Thanksgiving Day

God, Creator of all,
in our Thanksgiving Day anthems
we sing our gratitude
for this planet earth, our home.
Help us to show that gratitude
by taking care of the earth
so that future generations,
our children and our children's children,
will want to sing their praises too.
Let all the people give thanks.
Amen.

58 Thanksgiving Sunday or Thanksgiving Day

God of gods,
during this Thanksgiving season
we confess our self-indulgence
even as we raise our hymns and anthems
of grateful praise.
Deliver us all from "idol" diversions
of the marketplace,
the sports arena,
the theater,
and of the self;
and use our music to help us confront cries
for a more just and equitable order.
To this end we sing and pray, in Christ's name.
Amen.

(Adapted from *Novum Organum*, by Francis Bacon, 1561–1626)

59 Christ the King Sunday

Today we sing
of your kingdom, God
your kingdom of peace:
We sing with gratitude
that your kingdom is here;
with faith, that it is within us;
with love, that it is for all;
with hope, that it is coming still.
We offer our songs
for our Prince of Peace,
Jesus Christ.
Amen.

(Inspired by Luke 17:21 and 1 Corinthians 13:13)

60 Christ the King Sunday

Sovereign God, Ruler of all creation,
you have called us to be citizens
of Christ's realm
of love and justice and peace.
Let our eyes be to Christ,
that we may catch a vision of that realm.
Let our voices be to Christ,
that we may celebrate his rule.
Let our feet be to Christ,
that we may walk in his ways.
For his sake and his reign
we sing and pray.
Amen.

61 A Responsive Prayer

Leader: O God, open our lips:
Choir: And our mouths shall proclaim your praise.
Leader: O magnify God with me.
Choir: Let us magnify God together.
Leader: God's love endures forever.
Choir: God's love endures forever.

(Adapted from Psalm 51:15)

62

The heart, O God, this day rejoices.
In thanks we lift our hymns and voices.
Let our music rise to your ear.
Take joy, O God, in what you hear.
Amen.

(Inspired by "All My Heart Today Rejoices," by Paul Gerhardt, 1653;
trans. Catherine Winkworth, 1858)

63

Praise the Lord, for the Lord is good,
and greatly to be praised.
Praise the Lord, O House of Sydnor.*
Praise the Lord, O House of Walker.
Praise the Lord, O House of Benson.
Praise the Lord, O House of Bear.

Praise the Lord, O House of Izquierdo.
Praise the Lord, O House of Rennie.
Praise the Lord, O House of Lloyd.
Praise the Lord, O House of Jung.
Praise the Lord, O House of Kim.
Praise the Lord, O House of Frank.
Praise the Lord, O House of McCormick.
Let all who love the Lord, praise the Lord.
Amen.

(*Use at least a couple of names from each section of the choir.)

(Inspired by Psalm 145:3)

Prayers Asking God's Presence and Guidance

64

God, Source of all power,
we are trying our best
to be true to our pitches
as we sing
the sharps and flats today.
Help us try as hard
to be true to ourselves
and to you
in our worship
and in our lives.
We sing in the name of Christ,
who is our truth.
Amen.

(Inspired by *Hamlet*, by William Shakespeare)

65

Dearest Friend, give us today
thoughts of the heart, that we may know you;
ears of the heart, that we may hear you;
eyes of the heart, that we may see you;
sounds of the heart, that we may touch
the knowing, hearing, seeing hearts
of this congregation with our songs.
In Christ's name, we praise and pray.
Amen.

66

God,
we have been pounded for another week
with the sights and sounds
of traffic,
the workplace,
the marketplace,
the sports arena,
the media.
It is easy to lose
our perspective and ourselves.
Help us,
through the Word from our pastors
and the anthems and hymns we sing,
to see and hear Jesus
and find ourselves in serving one another
in your hustling, bustling, exciting world.
Travel with us this new week, God,
in Jesus' name.
Amen.

67

God, Love Divine.
Beginning and End of our music,
we pray that you will breathe your loving Spirit
into our songs today,
that they may enter every troubled heart.
By your love,
set our hearts at liberty
and our lives to your service.
In the name of Jesus Christ, our Alpha and Omega,
we sing and pray.
Amen

(Inspired by "Love Divine, All Loves Excelling," by Charles Wesley, 1747)

Prayers for Others

68

God, our Comforter,
some of us are cast down today,
weakened by a diet of
disappointment, sickness,
anger, death, and tears.
Feed us, God, day and night
with songs of faith, hope, and love
and so lift our spirits
in Christ's name.
Amen.

69

God, we sing "Hallelujahs" today,
not to please ourselves
but to praise you,
and for all who,
because of some bitter winter within or without,
can sing no song for themselves.
For them and for ourselves,
we raise our "Hallelujahs"
for your benediction.
Bless us as we sing,
in Christ's name.
Amen.

70

Great Healer God,
we may not preach like Peter,
nor pray like Paul,
nor sing like angels,
but we do need the balm from Gilead.
In our preaching,
our praying,
and our singing,
send your Holy Spirit, we pray,
that we may tell the love of Jesus,
revive the discouraged,
heal the sin-sick soul,
and make the wounded whole,
in the name of Jesus,
Amen.

(Adapted from Jeremiah 8:22 and "There Is a Balm in Gilead,"
African American spiritual)

Prayers of Commitment and Dedication

71

Not of ourselves do we sing, God,
but of Jesus Christ,
Lord and Savior,
and of ourselves as your children,
Christ's servants.
Hear our songs on this Lord's Day, in Christ's name.
Amen.

72

We are here, God,
choir and congregation.
Receive our presence
as a prayer for your presence among us.
Receive our reading of your Word,
preaching of your Word, and
listening to your Word
as a search for your promises and purposes.
Receive our hymns and anthems
as a longing for your benediction.
Amen.

73

Gracious God,
in Jesus Christ, you have given us your best gift.
Let his life be in our singing
to wake us up.
Let his light be in our singing
to help us see.
Let his love be in our singing
to stir us to care.
Let his peace be in our singing
to make us whole.
As we have received Christ from you,
so we give ourselves to you
as we sing for others
in Christ's name.
Amen.

74

Holy Spirit,
take the different notes we sing—
soprano, alto, tenor, bass,
and our different rhythms,
and help us sing together
with one heart and voice,
that your Word may be clear and compelling
to all who worship here this day.
In the name of Christ, we pray.
Amen.

75

God, we bring
a little thing:
a song,
a gift
we gladly sing.
Amen.

Special Days and Seasons

76 Advent

Emmanuel, God with us:
Come into our singing as joy.
Come into our singing as hope.
Come into our singing as love.
Come that the world may know
the joy and hope and love
of Christ and his rule.
So come, Emmanuel, come.
Amen.

(Inspired by "O Come, O Come, Emmanuel," ancient antiphons from Advent
Vespers translated by John Mason Neale, 1851, and others)

77 Advent

Eternal God,
our times are in your hands—
the time to sing, the time to keep silent.
We have rehearsed our songs.
Now we pause for prayer.
From this moment of silence,
may we go forth
to meet the needs of this congregation,
and our own needs,
with timely hymns and anthems.
We pray in the name of Jesus Christ,
whom you sent in the fullness of time.
Amen.

(Inspired by Ecclesiastes 3:1-8)

78 Advent

Merciful God,
it must amuse you
to hear us sing
Mary's Magnificat today.
After all,
we are the rich and powerful,
not the hungry or humble of this world.
Yet still we sing.
Do not send us away empty.
Remember your promises to your people.
Help us use our affluence and influence
with compassion and justice
and as much enthusiasm

as we have shown
in singing Mary's song
and honoring her Son,
in whose name, we pray.
Amen.

(Inspired by the "Canticle of Mary," Luke 1:46-55)

79 Advent

As we continue
our Christmas journey
toward Bethlehem, God,
let your Word and Spirit
be map and sign to us,
making clear the roadway
through all the seasonal distractions,
disturbances, and shopping malls
to the manger.
Give to us carols of repentance,
renewal, and rejoicing,
as we rendezvous with the Christ Child,
in whose name
we journey, sing, and pray.
Amen.

80 Advent

God of Peace,
minister not to our Christmas wants,
but to our needs.
Above all, give us the gift of discernment
that we may know and do
what will bring us inner peace
and peace in the world.
To that end,
we raise our Christmas carols to you
in the name of Jesus Christ, the Prince of Peace.
Amen.

81 Christmas Eve

As usual, God,
we have been very busy this Advent season,
getting, spending, partying.
It is difficult even for us Christians
to find room for the Christ Child today.
Give us a Christ-song for our hearts and lives,
so that the Christ Child may have a place
in all the rooms we enter this season of the year.
In Christ's name, we sing our Noels.
Amen.

82 Christmas Eve

God of many sounds,
you have spoken to us
in thunder from the mountain
and in a still, small voice;
through a choir of angels
and the cry of a babe in a cradle.
Speak to us now,
that our singing and music
may move our congregation
to hear and respond
to your Word and Spirit.
Amen.

(Inspired by Exodus 19:16-18; 2 Kings 19:11-13; and Luke 2)

83 Christmas Eve

We know we are not angels, God,
but we pray
you will make what we sing
sound like an angel chorus,
that our music may lift up
and inspire your people this day.
We ask this in Christ's name.
Amen.

84 Christmas

Christmas God,
we sing the angels' song of peace
and long for health and wholeness in our lives.
You know our condition:
we are as busy as innkeepers,
lonely as shepherds,
anxious as Mary and Joseph,
fearful as Herod,
restless as the wise men,
helpless as little children.
Give us the peace we need, God,
an inner peace that the world cannot give or take away.
We sing and pray
in the name of the Prince of Peace.
Amen.

(Inspired by Luke 2:1-20 and Matthew 2:1-11)

85 Christmas

God, hear our prayer as your children.
Amid all the diversions of this Christmas season,
help us to remember what is important:
you came to us as a little child,
you lived among us,
you live among us still,
you love each one of us.
Help us to sing with childlike faith and delight
in the name of the Christ Child.
Amen.

(Inspired by Luke 2 and Mark 10:13-16)

86 Christmas

God, as your congregation and choir,
we continue our Christmas pilgrimage,
let not the glitter and glitz of Christmas
blind us to the guiding star;
nor the season's cacophony
deafen us to the angels' chorus;
nor our frequent comings and goings
confuse our vision
of what Christmas is meant to be.
Rather, let your gift of Christ
be the light, truth, and peace
of our pilgrim way.
We sing and pray in his name.
Amen.

87 Christmas

God of holy love,
in this Christmas season,
help us cherish
all the words
and all the songs
of the manger scene,
and like Mary,
ponder them
in our hearts and lives.
In the name of the Christ Child,
we sing and pray.
Amen.

(Inspired by Luke 2:19)

88 Christmas Communion

Almighty God,
today you come to us in the infant Jesus,
the meekest of kings,
the lowliest of lords.
We come to his manger
and to the communion table
to celebrate his life, death, and resurrection for us.
We come with a sense of joy and peace and hope
that all the Caesars and Herods of this world
cannot give or take away.
We sing our noels in gratitude for the Risen Christ,
our King of kings and Lord of lords.
Amen.

(Inspired by John 14:27)

89 Christmas Communion

God of hope and joy,
you embrace us all in your love
as we gather at this Lord's Table.
By the power of your Word and Spirit,
let our Christmas songs express
the range, the length,
the breadth, the depth,
the height of your love
in Christ Jesus, our Lord and Savior.
Amen.

(Inspired by Ephesians 3:18-19 and "O Love, How Deep,"
fifteenth-century Latin text, translated by
Benjamin Webb and John Mason Neale, 1851)

90 Christmas Past, Present, and Future

God of Christmas past,
we sing in gratitude for every remembrance
of your love for us as your people.
God of Christmas present,
we sing in faith that you will continue to love us
and help us face life's challenges.
God of Christmas future,
we sing in hope that you will give us courage
for the living of the coming year.
So, God, bless us, every one,
Amen.

(Inspired by *A Christmas Carol*, a story by Charles Dickens, 1812–1870)

91 Last Sunday of the Year

Patient God,
who has been ever present with us
through all the changes and chances
of our fleeting years,
we praise and thank you.
On this last Sunday of the old year,
some of us are uncertain and uneasy
about what lies ahead.
Let the Christmas carols we have sung,
so full of purpose and promise,
echo in our hearts
that we may live faithful and fruitful lives
in the new year.
So we sing and pray, in Christ's name.
Amen.

92 Last Sunday of the Year

God, on this last Sunday of the old year,
we sing hymns and anthems
of faith and hope
for all those in the race of life
who feel like they are
running out of excuses,
running out of patience,
running out of health,
running out of time,
running out of songs.
Help all of us catch our wind,
keep the faith,
and run a good race of life.
So let Jesus run and sing with us
during this New Year.
Amen.

(Inspired by 2 Timothy 4:7)

93 New Year's Day

God of our lives,
of the past,
of the coming years,
through all the circling years,
we trust in you.
Let our music
for this year
say
Amen and Amen.

(Inspired by "God of Our Life," by Hugh Thomson Kerr, 1916)

94 New Year's Day

Here we are again, God,
on the first Sunday of a New Year.
We find ourselves between
then and there,
and here and now,
in our own age of anxiety.
Be with us on this day of new beginnings,
and give us Christ-songs
for the open road before us.
Amen.

(Inspired by For the Time Being, by W. H. Auden, 1944)

95 New Year's Day

God of the coming year,
give us old and new songs to sing,
and with each song,
firmer faith,
greater love,
brighter hope,
in Christ's name
and for your world.
Amen.

96 Epiphany

God of all nations,
on this Sunday of Epiphany,
we follow the Christ-star,
as did the Magi,
and, like them,
bring gifts for the Christ Child:
the gold of allegiance,
the frankincense of adoration,
the myrrh of self-sacrifice,
and hymns and anthems
of joy and gratitude.
Be with us in our pilgrimage, we pray.
Amen.

(Inspired by Matthew 2:1-11)

97 Epiphany

God, from whom all light comes,
today we still follow the Christ-star,
the brightest and best
of all your stars.
May it continue
to illumine the way
through the storm and stress
of our dark days.
May the burdens of our journey be lightened
with Christ-songs of joy and hope.
Shine, Christ Jesus, shine.
Amen.

(Inspired by "Brightest and Best of the Sons of the Morning,"
by Reginald Heber, 1811)

98 Epiphany

Enliven our singing, God,
by your Word and Spirit,
that our hymns and anthems
may pass from voice to voice,
from heart to heart,
from life to life,
as a lively witness
to your love for us and the world.
In Christ's name, we rejoice.
Amen.

99 Epiphany

To you, dear Christ, the world we bring.
For this, our world, we gladly sing
your life, your truth, your way.

(Inspired by John 14:6 and "Christ for the World We Sing,"
by Samuel Wolcott, 1813–1886)

100 Epiphany

God of grace,
whose praise we raise in this hour,
bless every testimony made to
your name,
your kingdom,
your will,
in the silence of our hearts,
in word and song,
and in daily lives,
that all the world may know
Jesus Christ as Lord,
and give thanks.
Amen.

101 Epiphany

We hear your call, God:
Go, sing it from my choir loft!
Go, sing it from my church steeples!
Go, sing it from my housetops and my tallest building!
Go, sing it from my highest mountain!
Jesus Christ is Lord!
Inspire us to answer your call
with our singing!
Amen.

(Adapted from "Go Tell It on the Mountain," African American spiritual)

102 Baptism of a Child

Great and gracious God,
we sing praises to you for our creation,
for settling us in families,
and for giving us children like Jane* to love.
We praise you also
for sending us Jesus
to live for us, die for us,
and give us hope through the resurrection.
Little Jane* knows nothing of this now,
but just as we have come to love one another
because you first loved us in Christ,
so may she come to know you and sing your praise.
Let your benediction rest upon her,
upon her mother, father, and family,
and upon all of us
who now welcome her
into your household of faith, hope, and love.
In Christ's name,
Amen.

(* Substitute the name of the child to be baptized.)

(Inspired by 1 John 4)

103 Baptism of a Child

As we baptize Rachel,*
we sing "Jesus loves me" for her,
but also for ourselves,
renewing our own baptismal vows.
We who are weak, God,
pray to you who are strong,
asking that you help us and help Rachel*
to grow in faith, hope, and love.
We sing in the name of Jesus,
who lived and died for us all.
Amen.

(* Insert the name of the child to be baptized.)

(Inspired by "Jesus Loves Me," by Anna B. Warner, 1860)

104 Baptism of a Child

God of all families,
as we baptize Chahnwon Thomas Kim* today,
we sing with joy.
In Christ there is no east or west,
no south or north,
but one great fellowship of love,
throughout the whole wide earth.
Bless Chahnwon,* child of the covenant.
Bless Jae Jun and MiLa,* parents in the covenant.
Bless us, godparents in the covenant,
and help us keep our promise to pray for Chahnwon,*
and nurture him in faith, hope, and love.
In Christ's name, we sing and pray.
Amen.

(* Substitute the name of the child to be baptized and his or her parents.)

(Inspired by "In Christ There Is No East or West," by John Oxenham, 1908)

105 Baptism

Baptize us again, God,
by the power of your Word and Spirit
and all the music we sing today.
Baptize every text,
every note, every measure,
every hymn and anthem,
that our music may belong to you
and be a blessing to this congregation.
So baptize each of our hearts
that we may rise up in your service
with Jesus Christ, our Lord.
Amen.

106 Communion

Today, God,
we remember you
in bread and wine,
in word and song.
Today, God,
please remember us,
for Christ's sake.
Amen.

107 Communion

We come to your table again, Lord.
Let us break bread together on our knees.
Let us drink wine together on our knees.
Let us sing hymns together on our knees.
O Lord, have mercy on us.

(Adapted from "Let Us Break Bread Together," African American spiritual)

108 Communion

Gracious God,
this is the hour of banquet and song;
the heavenly table for us spread.
Here let us feast, and feasting, still prolong
the joyous sound of living wine and bread.
Amen.

(Adapted from "Here, O My Lord, I See You Face to Face,"
by Horatius Bonar, 1855)

109 Martin Luther King, Jr. Day

Almighty God,
Governor of all nations,
we thank you
for reconciling us to you
and to one another
through your love in Jesus Christ.
You have commissioned us
to use our music
to proclaim this good news
to those who live without

such knowledge,
such faith,
such hope in your love.
Use us,
and strengthen us,
as we seek to be your ambassadors
in this world.
In Christ's name, we sing.
Amen.

(Inspired by 2 Corinthians 5:20)

110 Ecumenical Sunday or Week of Christian Unity

God, before whom
the whole family in heaven and earth sings,
root us and ground us in your love,
that we may know and sing
with Christians everywhere
the length and breadth,
the height and depth
of the love of Christ.
Let our love songs rise up
and shape our daily lives,
so others may know the fullness of your Spirit,
in whose power we sing and pray.
Amen.

(Inspired by Ephesians 3:18-19 and "O Love, How Deep, How Broad, How High,"
fifteenth-century Latin; translated by Benjamin Webb and John Mason Neale, 1851)

111 A Stormy Sunday

The weather outside is frightful, God:
gusty winds,
freezing temperatures,
ice and snow.
It was not easy to get here
for our ministry of music,
but we came,
remembering that you have made
even this day to give to us.
So be with us this morning, God:
fill us with the wind of your Spirit;
warm our hearts;
make our sins white as snow;
and help us walk in your ways.
In Christ's name,
we offer our prayers and praise.
Amen.

112 Valentine's Day

God of the open heart,
as we lift our voices to you,
we also offer up our hearts:
our faint hearts,
our broken hearts,
our cold hearts,
our sad hearts,
our hopeful hearts.
Make our hearts glad
with the joy of your love

for the living of our days.
We pray in Christ's name.
Amen.

(Inspired by Ezekiel 11:19*a*)

113 Valentine's Day

Loving God,
you have taught us
that we cannot sing to the heart
unless we sing from the heart.
Fill us with the power
of your Word and Spirit,
that what we sing,
and how we sing
may warm the hearts and change the lives
of those who worship here this day.
Amen.

Spring
Prayers of Praise and Thanksgiving

114 An Antiphonal Prayer

Leader: The Creator's praise we gladly sing.
Choir: Alleluia!
Leader: In cheerful sound all voices raise.
Choir: Alleluia!
Leader: The Redeemer's name we gladly sing.
Choir: Alleluia!
Leader: And fill the world with joyful praise.
Choir: Alleluia!

115

Praise God, Maker of heaven and earth.
Let the budding trees
praise you.
Let the sprouting grass
praise you.
Let the blooming bushes
praise you.
Let the purple pansies
praise you.
Let the singing birds
praise you.
Let this congregation and choir
praise you.
Let the whole order of creation
praise you for spring!
And let the people say:
Amen!

(Inspired by Psalm 147)

116

Amazing God,
whose grace first taught our hearts to sing,
now hear the prayers we raise,
and fill with grace the songs we bring,
this hour we come to praise.
Amen.

(Inspired by "Amazing Grace," by John Newton, 1779)

117

God,
may the power of your spirit
inspire our worship this day:
praise in words singing,
praise in tunes ringing,
praise for songs springing,
fresh from your Word.
In Christ's name, we praise.
Amen.

(Inspired by "Morning Has Broken," by Eleanor Farjeon, 1931)

118

Sing the birds down
from nest and tree,
Sing the flowers up
from seed and soil,
Sing through your children, God,
thankful for spring.
Amen.

119

God of the lilies of the field,
who has promised to give us
all that we need,
be with us now as we robe to sing.
Clothe us in suitable garments
for worship and service:
faith and forgiveness,
love and forbearance,
hope and gratitude,
that all we sing and do
may be in praise of you.
In Christ's name, we pray.
Amen.

(Inspired by Matthew 6:28-30. The metaphor of being "clothed" with abstract
qualities appears several times in the Psalms and elsewhere in the Bible.)

120

God,
we sing
e e cummings today
we thank you
for everything that is natural
the leaping greenly spirit of trees
the touching
tasting
seeing
hearing
breathing
we thank you God

for everything which is infinite
which is you
which is yes
which is Christ.
Amen.

(Inspired by "i thank You, God," by e e cummings)

121

God, open the inward heart, that we may delight in
you;
the inward eye, that we may see you;
the inward ear, that we may hear you;
the inward voice, that we may sing your praise.
In Christ's name, we pray.
Amen.

122

Christ,
through our hymns and anthems
we reach out to touch
the hem of your garment.
Do not put us off.
Accept our praise
as an expression
of our faith and hope
and of our need
for your healing touch.
Bless us now, as you did
that faithful woman so long ago.
Let the choir sing:
Amen.

(Inspired by Luke 8:43-48)

123

God,
we do not sing
to hear the congregation exclaim, "How beautiful!"
Rather, we sing
that worshipers may
see Christ and affirm, "The Way!"
hear Christ and confess, "The Truth!"
follow Christ and exclaim, "The Life!"
To that end, accept our praise.
In Christ's name, we sing.
Amen.

(Inspired by John 14:6)

Prayers Asking God's Presence and Guidance

124

Jesus,
let the music of our longing hearts
be our song today.
Sing with each of our sections,
that all who gather to worship
may know your presence
through our music.
Sing in all our hearts and lives, we pray.
Come, Lord Jesus, come.
Amen.

(Inspired by "Jesus, Thou Joy of Loving Hearts," attr. Bernard of Clairvaux,
1091–1153; trans. Ray Palmer, 1858)

125

God,
as you have clothed
the trees and bushes this spring
so fit us with garments
suitable for worship.
Robe us with
faith and forgiveness,
compassion and justice,
hope and expectation.
that so robed, we may sing to you
in spirit and in truth
and in Christ's name.
Amen.

126

Oh, what a beautiful morning
to sing your praise, great God!
We who have gathered here come with many needs:
Some of us may feel invigorated and on top of it all.
Give us songs of gratitude and service.
Some may feel down and out, despite the beauty of the
morning.
Give us songs to lift our spirits and give us strength.
Some may just keep plodding on, day in and day out.
Give us songs of assurance that our plodding is not in
vain.
Make this a beautiful day for us all.
Let the choir sing:
Amen!

127

Christ,
as you are ready to teach,
make us ready to learn.
Teach us
why we sing,
what to sing,
how to sing new songs
for worship and our every condition.
Come, Christ Jesus.
Come.
Amen.

128

God of steadfastness and encouragement,
keep us from being preoccupied
with Martha work:
practicing the organ,
rehearsing hymns and anthems,
robing, fixing our hair,
getting into the choir loft.
Show us the one thing needful—
that we listen,
and help this congregation listen,
like Mary,
to Jesus, in whose name
we do our Martha work,
and sing and pray.
Amen.

(Inspired by Luke 10:38-42)

129

Today, God, as we sing about Jesus
and the man who could not see,
we thank you for the sight
that enables us to enjoy one another
and the grandeur of your creation.
May we also see ourselves
through the eyes of Jesus,
and share his vision
for the persons we may become.
Help us to keep our eyes firmly focused on him,
that we may follow him with joy and hope.
So open our eyes
and help us sing today.
Amen.

(Inspired by John 9)

Prayers for Others

130

God,
in this spring season
use what we sing as a choir
to sow the seeds
of faith, hope, and love
in the hearts of this congregation.
Bring forth the fruits
of your Word and Spirit
in our day-by-day relationships.
So use our ministry of music
in Christ's name.
Amen.

(Inspired by Matthew 13:1-23; Mark 4:1-20; Luke 8:5-15; and Galatians 5:22-23)

131

Signs of your goodness, God,
surround us on this beautiful day.
How can we keep from singing?
Some who worship with us today
have never found their singing voice,
or have lost it.
Others feel they have nothing to sing about.
Fill us with your joy and peace
that we may sing
for those who have no voice or heart
to sing for themselves.
Let the love they hear in our songs
set their hearts to singing too.
In Christ's name,
we offer our music today.
Amen.

(Inspired by "My Life Flows on in Endless Song," attr. Robert Lowry, 1860)

132

Do not scatter our music
on the March-wind, God.
Carry it on the Christ-wind
into the hearts and lives
of the people gathered here.
Carry it beyond these walls to all people,
that they may hear and believe,
and have life abundant.
To that end we offer our Christ-songs
today.
Amen.

133

Christ Jesus,
once you took a few loaves and fish
to feed your followers.
Today, take our simple words and notes,
bless them, amplify them,
and feed this congregation
with your presence and love.
So come, generous Lord.
Amen.

(Inspired by Matthew 14:13-21; Mark 6:30-44; Luke 9:1-17; and John 6:1-13)

134

Compassionate God,
you know the names and needs
of all who gather here today—
a disturbed child,
a prodigal son or daughter,
a troubled Zacchaeus,
a repentant Mary Magdalene,
an uncommitted, rich young ruler,
a cautious Nicodemus,
an anxious Mary or Martha,
a proud Pharisee,
persons in all circumstances of life.
Let your Word and Spirit
minister to each one
through our music this day.
In Christ's name,
we sing and pray.
Amen.

(Inspired by Mark 9:14-29; Luke 15:11-32; Luke 19:1-10; Mark 14:3-9; 15:40; 16:1;
Luke 18:18-23; John 3:1-8; Luke 10:38-42; and Matthew 19:3)

135

Love Divine,
all loves excelling,
you are our life and liberty,
the beginning and end of all our singing.
Breathe your loving-kindness
into every song we sing,
that it may bring healing and comfort
to every troubled breast.
We pray and sing in the name
of your unbounded love.
Amen.

(Inspired by "Love Divine, All Loves Excelling," by Charles Wesley, 1747)

136

God,
let your Word and Spirit
. knead a little yeast
into our music today
to lift our hearts,
raise up this congregation,
and spread your rule of love
to all your children everywhere.
Let the choir say:
Amen and Amen.

(Inspired by Luke 13:21)

137

Christ, you healed all manner of sickness
when you walked among us.
Come again,
and use our music as a healing salve
to help the deaf hear,
the blind see,
and the lame walk
through repentance and renewal
to wholeness of life.
Continue your healing ministry among us.
Amen.

(Inspired by Luke 7:22)

Prayers of Commitment and Dedication

138

You never weary, Lord, of hearing your children;
let us never weary of singing your praise.
You never weary, Lord, of doing us good;
let us never weary of serving you.
Let the choir say:
Amen.

(Adapted from John Wesley, 1703–1791)

139

Righteous One,
we do not gain your attention
by singing *forte* or *mezzo forte*,
or even *fortissimo*.
You regard only the humble and contrite heart
and the life of justice.
Today we sing our praises *forte-piano*,
with humility, repentance,
and grateful hearts,
dedicating ourselves to your service.
In Christ's name, we sing.
Amen.

(Inspired by Micah 6:8)

Special Days and Seasons

140 Ash Wednesday

Merciful God,
Searcher of all hearts,
today we do not sing as the Pharisee,
but as the Publican,
praying for humble and contrite hearts,
that our singing and living
may be an acceptable service to you.
Send us out of this place
into our homes and into the world,
justified and grateful for your mercy.
In the name of Jesus, our Teacher, we sing.
Amen.

(Inspired by Luke 18:9-14 and Psalm 51:15-17)

141 Communion in Lent

Compassionate Christ,
who long ago
ate and drank with publicans and sinners,
you make us bold to ask
that you eat and drink
and sing with us today,
even though
we too fall short of your goodness.
Let your love dispel
all that is wrong in our lives,
and in the world in which we live.
To that end,
we break the bread,
raise our cups,
and offer our praise to you.
So eat, drink, and sing with us,
we pray.
Amen.

(Inspired by Mark 2:15-17)

142 Lent

Healer God,
whose heart has known the pain of the cross,
we gather as your family
with all our
body aches,
headaches,
heartaches.
Soothe us with the songs we sing.
Make us healers in this aching world.
In Christ's name, we sing and pray.
Amen.

143 Lent

Merciful God,
we continue our Lenten watch,
penitent,
confessing our secret sins,
our whispered sins,
the crying sins of our world.
You know them all before we confess them.
Therefore, in our worship and singing
we center on you
in awe of your glory,
your patience,
your forgiveness—
the new beginnings you provide us through Jesus
Christ,
in whose name we confess and sing.
Amen.

144 Lent

What language shall we borrow
to praise you, Dearest Friend?
Today we borrow
Mozart's music
and Latin, a language not quite our own.
Inspire our singing
that this music of Mozart
and these Latin words
may be a blessing to our congregation
and an acceptable service of praise to you.
In the name of Jesus, we sing.
Amen.

(Inspired by "O Sacred Head, Now Wounded," Medieval Latin attributed to
Bernard of Clairvaux, 1091-1153; German paraphrase by Paul Gerhardt, 1656;
trans. James Waddell Alexander, 1830)

145 Passion/Palm Sunday

Surprising God,
on this Palm Sunday,
we remember, in song,
Christ's entry into Jerusalem,
not as a Warrior King,
but as the King of Love.
Confound our ordinary ways.
Confront us with love.
Confirm us in faith.
Make "Hosanna" our daily song,
and hope our life,
in the name
of our triumphant Savior.
Amen.

(Inspired by Matthew 21:1-9; Mark 11:1-10; and Luke 19:28-38)

146 Passion/Palm Sunday

Compassionate God,
you have invited us to walk with Christ
on this Passion Week pilgrimage
through our music.
Be with us
as we descend from the heights of Hosanna
to the depths of despair,
as we move through despair and sorrow
to comfort and belief,
as we go through the valley of the shadow of death
to resurrection and new life with Christ.
May our pilgrim songs
be songs of great expectations
as we follow Christ along the way.
In his name, we pray.
Amen.

147 Passion/Palm Sunday

Christ Jesus, today we sing
of the tears of sorrow you sowed
when you rode into Jerusalem.
May they bring forth in us
a harvest of repentance
and new life of faith, hope, and love.
So refresh our discipleship, we pray.
Amen.

(Inspired by Luke 13:33-35 and 19:41-44)

148 Passion/Palm Sunday

Ride, Christ, ride
into our lives today.
Reign over us,
not because of the palms we wave,
not because of the hosannas we sing,
but because of your gracious love.
To this end,
we lift our voices in joyful praise.
Amen.

(Inspired by Matthew 21:1-11; Mark 11:1-10; Luke 19:28-38; and John 12:12-18)

149 Passion/Palm Sunday

Christ, our Prince of Peace.
ride into Richmond* this day.
Give us the will and power
not only to wave palms

and sing psalms,
but to seek peace for this city
in which we live and move
and have our being.
So we sing in your name.
Amen.

(* Substitute the name of your own community.)

(Inspired by Mark 11:1-10 and Acts 17:28)

150 Passion/Palm Sunday

Lord Jesus,
you rode into Jerusalem
as the crowd cheered, "Hosanna!"
You wept over the city,
and cleaned out the temple.
Today, we will sing our hosannas,
and you will weep over our city,
and over us.
Clean out
all unloving thoughts and intentions
from the hearts of those of us
who gather in this house of worship.
Turn our concerns instead to the peace
of your city and world,
for which you died and rose again.
Hosanna!
Amen.

(Inspired by Luke 19:41-44; Matthew 21:12-13; Mark 11:15-19; Luke 19:45-47; and
John 2:13-17)

151 Communion on Maundy Thursday

Christ Jesus, we sing again
of Gethsemane and Golgotha;
of Judas, who betrayed you with a kiss,
and Peter, who denied you.
Like them, we will share your bread and cup,
and sing a hymn with you;
Keep us from betraying your trust
or denying you, as they did.
Rather, let us
watch with you,
die with you,
and rise with you
to newness of life.
Alleluia!
Amen.

(Inspired by Luke 22:39-62)

152 Good Friday

We were there
when they crucified you, Lord,
We are here today
as you are crucified again
in every act of violence
we commit against one another,
against your creation,
and against that law of love
you have put in our hearts.
Trembling, we repent
on this Good Friday,
and pray that you will raise us up

with new hearts and lives.
So we sing and pray.
Amen.

(Inspired by "Were You There," African American spiritual)

153 Good Friday

Merciful Father,
by the power of your Spirit,
use the last dying words of our Lord,
which we sing
to slay all within us
that crucifies Jesus.
Out of shadow,
out of darkness,
out of death
bring hope,
light,
and life,
for Christ's sake.
Amen.

154 Good Friday

Compassionate Savior,
let us listen with our hearts
as well as our ears
to your words of forgiveness
from the cross
in our hymns and anthems.
Comfort us, and help us
to comfort one another
as we continue
our Easter pilgrimage.
Amen.

155 Easter

This is the day and hour
which you have made, God.
Help us to rejoice
and sing joyfully in it.
Alleluia!
Amen.

(Inspired by Psalm 118:24)

156 Easter

Christ Jesus,
on our Lenten pilgrimage
we have followed you through Gethsemane,
the Jerusalem gate, the Last Supper, and Golgotha.
Now we kneel at the empty tomb with Mary.
As you called her by name, so call us now:
Emily, Loretta, Elizabeth,
Jeff, Eric, Dan,
Alfrida, Jean, Barbara,
George, Ray, Bill.*
Call each person in this congregation by name as well.
Fill us all with hope for ourselves,
and hope for your Kingdom, present and coming.
So may we sing with thanksgiving
our Easter Hallelujah.
Amen.

(* Choose two or three members from each section of the choir to
name here.)

157 Easter

Christ of Gethsemane,
by your own suffering and sorrow
you have come to understand our needs.
When we sigh about our lives,
you sigh with us;
when we grieve our own sins,
you grieve with us;
when we weep about the world's sins,
you weep with us;
when we confront our own dying,
you stand with us.
You stand with us
When we long for victory over sin and death,
you share your triumph with us.
So we sing thanks, dear Friend, for life.
Amen.

158 Easter

Death, where is your sting?
Grave, where is your victory?
Thanks be to you, God,
who gives us the victory
through our Lord Jesus Christ!
Therefore,
we sing for joy,
abound in hope,
and live for your service,
grateful that we do not live in vain.
In the name of our resurrected Lord,
we sing and pray.
Amen.

(Inspired by 1 Corinthians 15:55, 57)

159 Easter

God,
keep us from missing Easter
on our Easter parades
under our Easter bonnets.
This is a day to sing
Christ's victory over sin and death,
your promise of the resurrection
and a new heaven and a new earth!
Therefore, let us joyfully parade,
and throw our bonnets high,
as we sing songs of faith, hope, and love!
Amen and Amen and Amen!

160 Easter

Great Heart of love,
on this glad Resurrection day,
let songs rise from our thankful hearts
as witness to our Resurrection joy.
Let the power of your Word and Spirit
melt the hard heart,
stir the doubting heart,
soothe the bruised heart,
mend the broken heart.
Make glad every heart as we sing
"Alleluia! Christ is risen!
Christ is risen indeed!"
Amen.

161 Easter

God of hope,
what a great work
you have wrought for us and the world
in raising Christ from the dead!
Help us this day
to trumpet hope,
preach hope,
sing hope,
live hope,
that the whole world may
hear and know and believe
in the Resurrection,
and wait with us
for your last trumpet
with hope and joy.
In the name of our Risen Lord,
we pray and sing.
Alleluia!
Amen.

162 Easter

God of life and death and new life,
our hymns and anthems
resound with "Hallelujahs" today.
Help us to sing them
humbly, gratefully, hopefully,
that you may not tire of our singing
but accept our great joy
on this glad Resurrection day!
We raise our Hallelujahs in Christ's name.
Amen.

163 Easter

Victorious God,
we sing today to the trumpet sounds
of your ultimate victory
over principalities and powers,
over the sin and death of this world.
Yet we still wait for that victory,
the fulfillment of your promises.
For the Time Being, help us to wait
in faith and hope and love.
Lead us in unique adventures with Christ,
our triumphant Lord.
Let the choir sing: Amen!
Amen and Amen.

(Inspired by *For the Time Being*, by W. H. Auden, 1944)

164 Communion on Easter

Come, Risen Christ.
Walk with us once more
along the Emmaus Road.
Open us afresh to the Scriptures
that our hearts may burn within us.
Share with us again
the bread and the cup.
Stay with us.
Do not depart.
As we sing our Easter carols,
let the power of your Word and Spirit
give us joy and hope,
and accompany us
on the road in your service.
Amen.

(Inspired by Luke 24:13-35)

165 A Rainy Sunday

Lord of all weather,
on this rainy Sunday morning
let your rainbow shine through
our psalms and hymns and spiritual songs
to reassure us of your constant love and care
as we pass through
all the storms and stress and strains
of our daily lives.
In the name of Christ, our bright hope, we sing.
Amen.

(Inspired by Genesis 9:12-17 and Revelation 14:3)

166 Mother's Day

God, on this Mother's Day,
we thank you for
mothers,
grandmothers,
and great-grandmothers,
and for all the songs
of faith, hope, and love
they taught us.
Through our songs of praise
help us to be godmothers
to one another today,
in Christ's name.
Amen.

167 Memorial Service

We sing today from the Brahms *Requiem*
our God.
We sing it in memory of John Brown,*
our pastor, preacher, leader, and friend;
for the comfort of his family,
and for ourselves.
We are all like the grass
that withers,
and the flowers of the field
that fade and die.
But thanks be to you, God,
for giving us the victory
through our Lord Jesus Christ,
and blessing all who die in the Lord!
We sing hopefully, joyfully, thankfully
in Christ's name.
Amen.

(* Substitute the name of the deceased.)

(Inspired by Isaiah 40:6-8; 1 Corinthians 15:57; and Revelation 14:13;
and *German Requiem* by Johannes Brahms)

168 Memorial Service

God, we pause today
to remember Myrtle Curtis,*
a faithful member of this congregation and choir.
We thank you for your musical gifts to her,
and her joy in sharing them with us.
Hear us now, as we raise our voices
in the music she loved,

knowing that she is singing with us
in your heavenly choir.
May our music comfort her family and friends
and all of us gathered here
to celebrate her life.
Fill us, we pray, with joy and peace
through our faith in the Risen Christ,
in whose name we sing.
Amen.

(* Substitute the name of a member of your choir or congregation.)

Summer
Prayers of Praise and Thanksgiving

169 An Antiphonal Prayer

Leader: Hymns of praise, now let us sing!
Choir: Alleluia!
Leader: Unto Christ, our heavenly King.
Choir: Alleluia!

170 A Responsive Prayer

Leader: O come, let us sing to God
        who loves us with a steadfast love.
**Choir: And shout with joy
        to the Rock of our salvation!**
Leader: Let us come into God's presence
        with thanksgiving.
Choir: And joyful songs of praise.

(Adapted from Psalm 89:1, 26 and Psalm 100)

171

On this sleepy summer morning, God,
wake us up and stretch us,
that we may rise and shine and sing
on this day you have made
and given to us for your praise.
So come, Holy Spirit, come!
Amen.

172

God, we gather this morning as a choir
because of our love for good music and singing,
but we do not gather simply to hear our own voices.
We sing that we might better hear your voice,
and praise you in the company of your people.
Accept our music and our singing
as our grateful devotion to you.
Let the choir say:
Amen!

173

From whence come our songs, O God?
From the night,
and its singing stars;
from a sunrise,
and a new day dawning.
From a mountain,
in its awesome majesty;
from a sandy beach,

the ocean's vast expanse.
From the smile of a happy child;
the tear of a lingering sorrow,
an act of kindness,
an offense graciously forgiven.
From a death swallowed up in hope
for new life with you.
All come from you, God,
Creator, Provider, Redeemer.
All come from you.
Amen.

174

Thank you, God,
for music—
the beautiful melodies and harmonies
that fill our hearts with joy.
Fill us also with your Word and Spirit
that we may remember
what we sing,
not simply our singing.
Thus we may praise you
in spirit and in truth.
Alleluia!
Amen.

(Adapted from *Confessions* by Augustine, A.D. 354–430)

175

Your eye is on the sparrow, God,
we know you watch over us:
Your eye is on the sparrow.
Christ's love inspires our trust.
Let the choir say:
Amen!

(Adapted from Matthew 10:31 and "His Eye Is on the Sparrow,"
by Mrs. C. D. Martin, 1906)

Prayers Asking God's Presence and Guidance

176

Source of life,
as we gather once again for worship,
come among us as Word and Spirit;
come among us in the presence of Christ;
for without your Word
our hymns will be worthless,
without your Spirit,
our anthems will be wingless,
without your promises in Christ,
we will be hopeless.
Come, Word and Spirit.
Come, Living Christ.
It is in your name that we pray.
Amen.

177

Jesus,
be here today in our worship.
Be in the pulpit,
in the readings, preaching,
and prayers of our pastors.
Be in the choir loft,
in our anthems
and in the hymns we sing
with the congregation.
Be in the world,
in the way we live and work
when we leave this hour with you.
Let the choir say:
Amen.

(Inspired by Matthew 18:20)

178

Ever-present God:
Be in our hearts
and in our feeling;
Be in our minds
and in our understanding.
Be in our mouths
and in our singing.
Be in our lives
and in our serving.
Be present with us
as we worship in Jesus' name.
Amen.

(Inspired by "God Be in My Head,"
from the sixteenth-century *Sarum Book of Hours*)

179

God, once again we gather
on this first day of the week
to confess to one another and the world
that you are the chief end
of all our singing and living.
In the coming week,
help us profess through our lives
what we sing with our lips,
and so glorify you in Christ's name.
Amen.

(Inspired by *Westminster Shorter Catechism*)

180

Faithful God,
we come here to worship and sing
because of the Good News of Jesus Christ,
news that we need to hear
over and over again.
Let your Spirit be heard in our singing
that our hymns and anthems may
carry this Good News to all who gather here.
We sing, in the name of Jesus Christ.
Amen.

181

God,
once again we gather in your house
to sing the old, old story
of Jesus and his love.
Inspire us
to sing it simply,
to sing it often,
to sing it always
as your faithful congregation and choir.
In Jesus' name we pray and sing and live.
Amen.

(Inspired by "I Love to Tell the Story," Katherine Hankey, 1866)

182

God of compassion,
as we pass through life's dry valleys,
quench our thirst
with songs of hope
from the well of your love.
Refresh us in the name of Christ,
your water of life.
Amen.

(Inspired by Ezekiel 37:1-6)

183

Divine Musician,
by the power of your Word and Spirit
direct us in our singing and
tune our hearts to your will,
that not only our hymns and anthems,
but also our lives
may be a harmonious
and constant
witness to you.
We pray and sing in Christ's name.
Amen.

184

Come, Jesus,
beloved Companion,
sing with us,
that this congregation may hear
not our voices,
but yours,
singing words
of comfort and challenge.
So come, Jesus,
come.
Amen.

185

Jesus,
Joy of our desiring:
be in our music.
Be the song
of our loving hearts.
Amen.

(Inspired by "Jesus, Joy of Our Desiring" by Martin Janus, 1661;
trans. Robert Seymour Bridges)

186

Help us worship today, O Master
with songs that only you can give,
songs that send a shining ray of hope
far down the future's broadening way;
songs that call us to lowly paths of service free.
O Master, sing with us, walk with us,
in this service.
Amen.

(Inspired by "O Master, Let Me Walk with Thee," by Washington Gladden, 1879)

187

God , Source of peace and harmony,
let the power of your Word and Spirit
tune up our off-key lives this morning.
As we are diligent in finding the right pitch
for our hymns and anthems,
may we also be concerned about using
your gifts of faith, hope, and love
to live together in the right key
as your people in the world.
Let the choir sing:
Amen and Amen.

188

God, Giver of all spiritual songs:
For life itself, give us a thankful song;
for our doubting, a faith song;
for our sadness, a glad song;
for our meanness, a love song;
for our anxiety, a hope song.
Make all our songs this day of days
Christ songs.
Amen.

189

How shall we sing your song, God,
by the waters of the James?*
Inspire us with songs
for the whole heart,
for the whole mind,
for the whole life,
in the name of your living water,
Jesus Christ, our Lord.
Amen.

(* Supply alternative phrase for your situation.)

(Inspired by Psalm 137:4 and John 4:10)

190

Word of God,
shape our words;
Love of God,
inspire our melodies and harmonies,
that the hymns and anthems we sing
may tell of your greatness,
and your gracious love
for all your children everywhere.
We sing in the name of Jesus Christ,
your Word and Love
made flesh.
Amen.

191

God, help us to sing
with one accord today—
humbly, lovingly,
compassionately,
hopefully, joyously—
so that everyone in this congregation
may be moved to confess
that Jesus Christ is Lord
in heart and head and life,
to your honor and glory.
Amen.

(Inspired by Philippians 2:9-11)

192

Life-giving God,
use the power of your Word and Spirit
to shape us,
and breathe life into us,
so that not just our mouths,
but our hearts and lives as well,
may bring forth songs
worthy of you.
Amen.

193

Arm us this day
with your Word and Spirit, O God,
and with songs of faith, hope, and love,
that we might take courage,
fight the good fight,
and keep the faith.
In the name of Christ,
our helmet, shield, and sword,
we pray.
Amen.

(Inspired by Ephesians 6:10-17)

194

God of hope,
fill our music,
with all joy and peace in believing,
that, by the power of your Word and Spirit,
it may resound
with faith, hope, and love.
In Christ's name, we sing.
Amen.

(Inspired by Romans 15:13)

195

Your joyful music leads us "Son-ward," God,
beyond the daily routine,
beyond the frustrations and anxieties of our personal
lives,
beyond the unruliness and unfairness of this world,
in the triumph song of life.
Teach us,
by your giving and forgiving,
how to love each other,
and make us victors in the midst of strife.
In the name of your Son, Jesus the Christ,
we pray and sing.
Amen.

(Adapted from "Joyful, Joyful, We Adore Thee," by Henry Van Dyke, 1907)

196

Lord, make us instruments
of your peace this day.
Where there is hatred, let us sing love;
where there is injury, pardon.
Where there is doubt, let us sing faith;
where there is despair, hope.
Where there is darkness, let us sing light;
where there is sadness, joy.
In such songs, may we too find peace.
Let the choir sing:
Amen.

(Adapted from a prayer by St. Francis of Assisi, 1181–1226)

197

O God,
give us
hymns
and anthems
and spiritual songs,
until our lives shall end;
and breath,
until our singing is done.
Amen.

(Adapted from the epitaph of Winifred Holtby)

Prayers for Others

198

God, our Comforter and our Strength,
let our song go forth to this congregation.
Confirm our faith,
and encourage us all
to strengthen the fainthearted
and comfort the afflicted,
rejoicing in the power of your Word and Holy Spirit.
We sing and pray in Christ's name.
Amen.

(Inspired by 1 Thessalonians 5:14)

199

Let our congregation praise you, God;
let all the congregations in this city praise you,
that all Richmond*
may know your name
and your saving grace,
and do your will.
So come to our troubled city, God,
in Christ's name.
Amen.

(* Substitute the name of your own community.)

200

God of all ages,
We sing to you as youngsters,
just exploring life's meaning.
We sing to you in our middle years,
carrying burdens of the day and nights.
We who are older sing to you
in the white winter of our years.
Give to us, we pray, songs appropriate
for every passage of life,
in the name of our companion,
Jesus Christ.
Amen.

201

If, dear Lord, you can use
our praise in singing,
to ease one life the aching,
to stop one heart from breaking,
then we will not have sung in vain.
Let the choir sing:
Amen and Amen.

(Adapted from a poem, "If I Could Stop One Heart from Breaking,"
by Emily Dickinson, 1864)

Prayers of Commitment and Dedication

202

Long-suffering God,
how patient you are
with the noise of our solemn assemblies,
Sunday after Sunday after Sunday.
And here we are again!
May the power
of your Word and Holy Spirit
transform us as we sing,
and make us willing
to serve you with our lives
as well as our lips.
So make our worship an acceptable sacrifice,
pleasing to your ears.
In Christ's name, we come.
Amen.

(Inspired by Amos 5:21)

203

Sovereign God,
you have called us
to be your choristers in this congregation.
Let our hearts be to you,
that we may know that you are God of all.
Let our eyes be to you
that we may catch a vision of your rule.
Let our voices be to you
that we may proclaim what we have heard and seen.
Let our feet be to you
that we may walk in your ways.
In Christ's name, we sing and pray
for the coming of your Kingdom.
Amen.

204

Creator God,
we sing YES to you
and your creation;
Redeemer God,
we sing YES to you
and your new creation,
Jesus Christ, our Lord and Savior.
We sing YES
for ourselves,
and those for whom
life has in some way been NO.
May our YES-songs
be a faithful witness
to your love!
Amen.

205

Creator God,
Source of all the music
in your rolling spheres
and our ringing ears,
we cannot withhold from you
that which is already yours,
that which you have given us
for our good.
Graciously receive
the fruit of our rehearsals,
that your music
may build up this congregation
and thus glorify you.
In the name of Christ,
your Song of Songs, we sing.
Amen.

(Inspired by "This Is My Father's World," by Maltbie D. Babcock, 1901)

206

God, our Guardian and Guide,
use our psalms and hymns and spiritual songs
not simply to delight the ear,
but to direct us and this congregation
in our duty to you and to one another.
So let the word of Christ
and the peace of Christ
dwell in our hearts.
Amen.

(Inspired by Colossians 3:15-17)

207

God,
our hands and fingers
give you musical skills,
our voices, words and notes;
our heads give you proficiency;
our hearts, love.
Receive these gifts, in Christ's name.
Amen.

208

Gracious God,
deliver us from cheap praise today.
Take our lives as well as our lips,
and make us a choir and congregation for others.
In the name of Christ who sacrificed himself for us,
we sing and pray and serve.
Amen.

(Inspired by Dietrich Bonhoeffer, 1906–1945)

Special Days and Seasons

209 Pentecost

Come to us, Spirit God, this Pentecost!
Come as mighty wind, not to blow us over
but to wake us up.
Come as fire, not to consume us

but to purify us.
Come as light, not to blind us
but that we, young and old, may see visions.
Come as mystic chords of music, not to divert
but to inspire us to your service
of faith and hope and love.
So come, Holy Spirit, come.
Amen.

(Inspired by Joel 2:28–32; Acts 2:1-21)

210 Pentecost

Holy Spirit, in whom
there is no north or south,
east or west,
it was on Pentecost
that you first taught our hearts to sing.
Now, we lift our voices,
with all our Christian sisters and brothers
under the northern and southern,
eastern and western skies.
Magnify our songs
that all your children,
in every tongue and every clime,
may know Christ
and the power of Christ's love.
Amen.

(Inspired by Galatians 3:28 and "In Christ There Is No East or West,"
by John Oxenham, 1908)

211 Pentecost

Ever-living God,
touch us today with the fire and wind
of your Holy Spirit.
Rekindle our devotion.
Retune our formal songs,
that our singing may not languish on our tongues.
Let our songs be a testimony to the Savior's love.
In Christ's name, we sing and pray.
Amen.

(Inspired by "Come, Holy Spirit, Heavenly Dove," by Isaac Watts, 1707)

212 Pentecost

God of all nations,
your Pentecostal fire burns still,
and spreads in Africa and Asia,
the Americas.
Kindle afresh that flame in us,
and unite our hearts and voices
with all who sing "Alleluia"
in every tongue, but
of one body, one Spirit, and one hope.
In Christ's name, we sing and pray. Amen.

213 Pentecost

Holy Spirit,
let your divine muse and music
vibrate in our memory
so they will be there for us
when we need them
in the coming week.
Come, Holy Spirit, come.
Amen.

214 Trinity Sunday

Triune God,
we sing your praise on this day:
We praise you
as God the Father,
Creator, Provider, Judge.
We praise you
as God the Son,
Redeemer, Lord, Companion.
We praise you
as God the Spirit,
Sanctifier and Comforter.
Let the whole world praise you,
Triune God.
Amen.

215 Children's Day

Not of ourselves alone do we sing today, God,
but of Jesus Christ, our Savior,
and ourselves as your children.
Hear us, in Christ's name.
Amen.

216 Children's Day

God, Source of all our great expectations,
help us sing and hear the Good News of Jesus Christ,
as if we were hearing and singing it for the first time.
Surprise us with joy once again.
Amen.

(Inspired by *Surprised by Joy*, by C. S. Lewis, 1898–1963)

217 Independence Day (Fourth of July)

Almighty God,
you call all the shining stars
and noisy nations by name!
Who are we,
that you should be mindful of us?
Yet you call each of us by name:
Cheryl, David, Lee,
Dan, Emily, Jim,
Margaret, Allen, Miri,
Alfred, Loretta,
Elizabeth, Mary,*
all your trusting children

of this congregation and choir!
Help us to sing and live
for the healing of the nations
in the name of Christ,
our guiding star.
Amen.

(* Substitute the names of members of your choir, using two from
each section.)

(Inspired by Psalm 8:4)

218 Independence Day (Fourth of July)

God of all peoples,
on this national holiday
we wave the red, white, and blue,
and raise our national hymns and anthems.
Help us remember
that it is you who has made us
a people of plenty, privilege, and pleasure.
Deliver us from national pride,
make us truly thankful,
and help us use our resources
to build a more compassionate,
equitable, and peaceful world
for all your peoples.
Make this a day of dedication,
not just another holiday.
In Christ's name, we pray.
Amen.

219 Independence Day (Fourth of July)

God of the nations,
on this Fourth of July
we sing our national hymns and anthems
and pledge again our allegiance.
We priase you,
not just for our country,
but for life itself.
We praise you,
not just for civil and religious liberties,
but for the freedom we know in Christ.
We praise you, also, for the happiness
that many of us enjoy.
Here and now, we pledge ourselves
to lead more compassionate and just lives,
to seek the happiness of all
for the health of our nation,
and in Christ's name.
To that end we sing and pray: Amen.

220 A Time of Drought

God,
as the parched earth reaches up for rain and
refreshment,
so our hearts thirst for you.
By the power of your Word and Spirit
fill us with songs of blessings
that our thirsty hearts may be satisfied.
In the name of Christ, water of life,
we sing.
Amen.

221 Communion

Day after day,
week after week, God,
you sustain us with food for our bodies,
and we are grateful.
Today, at this Lord's Table,
satisfy us
with soul-food,
soul-bread,
soul-wine,
soul-songs
for the coming days and weeks of our lives.
We sing in the name of our host,
Jesus the Christ.
Amen.

222 Communion

Christ Jesus, we gather with you at this table:
Blood of life, poured out for us,
forgive and transform us.
Bread of life, broken for us,
satisfy and strengthen us.
Song of life, sung for us,
come and celebrate with us
as we eat and drink in your name.
Amen.

223 Communion

Emmanuel,
we sing your songs
around your table today:
a song of Bethlehem,
of Nazareth and Galilee,
a song of Calvary
and the Emmaus road.
Feed our hearts and minds
so that we may sing
a song of Richmond,*
in your name,
during the coming week.
so come, Lord Jesus, come!
Amen.

(* Substitute the name of your community.)

(Inspired by "O Sing a Song of Bethlehem," by Louis Benson, 1889)

Index

225 Psalm References

227 References to Historical Church Figures

228 References to Poets and Authors

229 References to Composers of Larger Choral Works